Alabama

Rich Smith

Visit us at
www.abdopublishing.com

Published by ABDO Publishing Company, 8000 West 78th Street, Suite 310, Edina, Minnesota 55439 USA. Copyright ©2010 by Abdo Consulting Group, Inc. International copyrights reserved in all countries. No part of this book may be reproduced in any form without written permission from the publisher. The Checkerboard Library™ is a trademark and logo of ABDO Publishing Company.

Printed in the United States.

Editor: John Hamilton
Graphic Design: Sue Hamilton
Cover Illustration: Neil Klinepier
Cover Photo: iStock Photo
Interior Photo Credits: Alabama Department of Archives & History/Nathan Glick, Alamy, Amy Heatherington, AP Images, Birmingham Barons, Comstock, Corbis, David Olson, Getty, Granger Collection, Gunter Küchler, Huntsville Stars, iStock Photo, J.P. Lippincott and Co., Library of Congress, Mile High Maps, Mineral Information Institute, Mobile Bay Bears, Montgomery Biscuits, Mountain High Maps, NASA/Marshall Space Flight Center, National Oceanic and Atmospheric Administration, North Wind Picture Archives, One Mile Up, U.S. Forest Service, U.S. Postal Service, University of New Brunswick, and Walt Disney Pictures.

Statistics: State population statistics taken from 2008 U.S. Census Bureau estimates. City and town population statistics taken from July 1, 2007, U.S. Census Bureau estimates. Land and water area statistics taken from 2000 Census, U.S. Census Bureau.

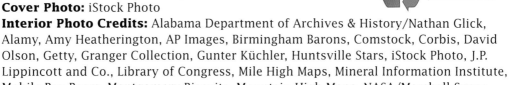

Manufactured with paper containing at least 10% post-consumer waste

Library of Congress Cataloging-in-Publication Data

Smith, Rich, 1954-
  Alabama / Rich Smith.
     p. cm. -- (The United States)
  Includes index.
  ISBN 978-1-60453-636-2
  1. Alabama--Juvenile literature. I. Title.

F326.3.S657 2010
976.1--dc22
                          2008050997

Table of Contents

The Heart of Dixie

Alabama is in the Deep South region of the United States. This region is often called Dixie. Alabama is a land of many natural wonders. There are gently flowing rivers, deep caves, pine forests, and low mountains. It has one of the country's longest natural rock bridges. And, a small part of the state has shoreline along the pleasant Gulf of Mexico.

Alabama in the early 1800s was part of the American frontier. Today, it is part of the "final frontier" because Alabama is where space missions are planned and readied.

Alabama is also a place of industrial importance. Americans more and more rely on the state for the cars they drive and for many of the other products they use. These include everything from electronics to steel and coal.

DeSoto Falls in Alabama's DeSoto State Park.

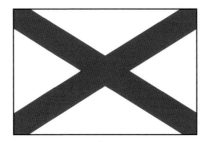

Quick Facts

Name: Alabama comes from the Choctaw (a Native American tribe) language. The name probably means "clearers of the thicket" or "gatherers of plants."

State Capital: Montgomery, population 204,086

Date of Statehood: December 14, 1819 (22nd state)

Population: 4,661,900 (23rd-most populous state)

Area (Total Land and Water): 52,419 square miles (135,765 sq km), 30th-largest state

Largest City: Birmingham, population 229,800

Nicknames: The Heart of Dixie, the Yellowhammer State, the Cotton State

Motto: We Dare Maintain Our Rights

State Bird: Yellowhammer

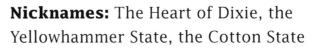

State Flower: Camellia

State Rock: Marble

State Tree: Southern Longleaf Pine

State Song: "Alabama"

Highest Point: Mount Cheaha in Talladega County, 2,407 feet (734 m)

Lowest Point: Gulf of Mexico, 0 feet (0 m)

Average July Temperature: 90°F (32°C)

Record High Temperature: 112°F (44°C), in Centerville on September 5, 1925

Average January Temperature: 49°F (9°C)

Record Low Temperature: -27°F (-33°C), in New Market on January 30, 1966

Average Annual Precipitation: 58 inches (147 cm)

Number of U.S. Senators: 2

Number of U.S. Representatives: 7

U.S. Postal Service Abbreviation: AL

Geography

Alabama is located in the southern United States. Its neighbor to the north is Tennessee. To the east is Georgia. South of the state are Florida and the Gulf of Mexico. Mississippi is next door to the west.

Alabama is shaped like a rectangle that is slightly smaller at the top than at the bottom. Alabama covers 52,419 square miles (135,765 sq km). It is the 30th-largest state.

Most of Alabama is a plain that gently slopes from the north to the south. The highest point is Mount Cheaha. It rises 2,407 feet (734 m) above sea level. It is located in the eastern half of the state's middle section. The lowest point is sea level, in the southwest corner where Alabama meets the Gulf of Mexico.

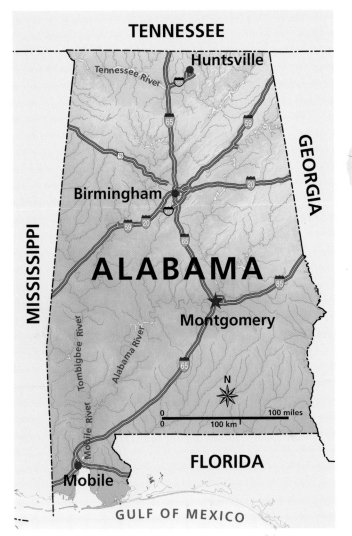

TENNESSEE

Tennessee River

Huntsville

65

59

78

GEORGIA

20

Birmingham

59 20

65

MISSISSIPPI

ALABAMA

65

Tombigbee River

Alabama River

Montgomery

65

N

0   100 miles
0   100 km

Mobile River

Mobile

FLORIDA

GULF OF MEXICO

Alabama's total land and water area is 52,419 square miles (135,765 sq km). It is the 30th-largest state. The state capital is Montgomery.

Alabama has four natural regions. Three of them are in the northern half of the state. The region in the far northwest is called the Appalachian Plateau. It is also sometimes called the Cumberland Plateau. It is a place of many low mountains. Next to it is the Ridge and Valley region. This area has mountains, too, but also miles of flat land between them. South of this is the Piedmont region. Here the mountains turn into small, rolling hills. The entire southern half of the state is known as the Coastal Plain.

The Tensaw River in southern Alabama.

The most important rivers are the Alabama, Tennessee, Tombigbee, Tensaw, and Mobile Rivers. The largest body of water completely within Alabama is Guntersville Lake.

Alabama has very good soil for farming. Beneath that soil are thick layers of limestone and dolomite.

Many deep caves exist in the hill and mountain areas. In the northwest corner is the longest natural rock bridge east of the Rocky Mountains.

A man stands in front of a skylit cave waterfall in northeastern Alabama. Many deep caves can be found in Alabama.

Climate and Weather

In 2005, Hurricane Katrina struck Mobile, Alabama.

Alabama's climate is mostly subtropical. This means its winters are mild and its summers are hot. The average January temperature is about 49° Fahrenheit (9°C). The average July temperature is about 90° Fahrenheit (32°C).

The reason Alabama has a subtropical climate is because it is so near the warm waters and moist air of the Gulf of Mexico.

The effects of the subtropical climate are strongest in the southern half of the state. For example, it rains more in the southern part than in the northern part. The average yearly rainfall throughout Alabama is about 58 inches (147 cm).

Being near the Gulf of Mexico also means that deadly hurricanes may lash the state with fierce winds and driving rain. More frequent than hurricanes in Alabama are tornadoes. And, more frequent than tornadoes are thunderstorms. Alabama has more days with thunderstorms than any other state.

Lightning rips across the sky above the Alabama capitol building.

Plants and Animals

Forests once covered much of Alabama. Farms and cities have since taken the place of many of them. But forests still exist. Many are quite large. They are filled mainly with pine trees. Also found in these forests are poplar, cypress, hickory, oak, gum, red cedar, southern white cedar, hemlock, hackberry, ash, and holly trees. Most common in the hot, humid Gulf Coast region are palm and palmetto trees.

Many kinds of shrubs grow in Alabama. These include mountain laurel, wisteria, rhododendron, and camellia. Camellia bushes produce a bloom so beautiful that Alabama decided to make it the state's official flower. Alabama also has many types of wildflowers. The state's official wildflower is the oak-leaf hydrangea.

The state's most important birds are the golden and bald eagle, osprey, hawk, black and white warbler, quail, duck, wild turkey, goose, and yellowhammer. Yellowhammer is the official bird of Alabama.

In the 1950s and 1960s, bald eagles were nearly gone from Alabama. However, through the efforts of scientists and volunteers in the past 25 years, nesting bald eagles have returned to the state.

Alabama is home to many kinds of animals. Among those in largest number is the white-tailed deer. Far fewer are elk, bear, panther, and bobcat. Beaver, muskrat, weasel, raccoon, opossum, rabbit, squirrel, red fox, gray fox, and armadillo are among other members of Alabama's animal kingdom.

Some Alabama animals are endangered. These include the wood stork, red-belly turtle, Alabama beach mouse, gray bat, finback whale, and humpback whale.

Thriving in Alabama's rivers, lakes, and streams are many fish, such as bream, shad, bass, and sucker.

Tarpon is Alabama's state fish.

Found in the waters of the Gulf of Mexico along the Alabama shoreline are pompano, redfish, bonito, and tarpon. Tarpon is the state's official fish.

A small population of black bears are found in southern Alabama.

Bobcat

Wood Stork

Red Fox

History

Among the first to live in Alabama was a group of people known as the Mound Builders. They were famous for creating hills 10 to 40 feet (3 to 12 m) high upon which they held ceremonies of various kinds.

Next came the Creek, Cherokee, Choctaw, and Chickasaw Native American tribes. They were mostly farmers, potters, and traders who began settling in Alabama during the Middle Ages.

An Alabama Native American village surrounded by a palisade (wooden fence).

The first European to reach Alabama was Alonzo Alvarez de Piñeda of Spain in 1519. He came by way of the Gulf of Mexico.

In 1540, Hernando de Soto and his soldiers fought with Indian warriors led by Chief Tuscaloosa in present-day Alabama.

In 1540, Hernando de Soto traveled by land through Alabama. He brought an army of 600 Spanish soldiers called conquistadors. Several times after that, Spain tried to colonize Alabama. But each attempt failed.

The first country to successfully colonize Alabama was France, in 1702. They started a Mobile River settlement about 30 miles (48 km) inland from the Gulf of Mexico. About 50 years later, France went to war with Great Britain and lost Alabama. Britain in turn lost the southwestern part of Alabama to Spain in 1780 during the American War of Independence. It lost the rest of Alabama to the United States three years later. In 1814, the United States took over Spain's piece of Alabama.

Alabama became a state in 1819. It was the 22nd state to join the Union. Settlers quickly flooded in. Many became farmers. Some chose to grow cotton because Alabama's soil was perfect for it. Large cotton farms called plantations sprang up. But the job of tending and picking the cotton belonged to slaves.

Most of the slaves were the grown-up children, grandchildren, and great-grandchildren of Africans brought as captives to the southern colonies of America.

Slaves picked cotton on Alabama plantations in the 1800s.

On February 18, 1861, Jefferson Davis became president of the Confederate States of America in Mobile, Alabama.

Cotton became such a big business for Alabama that the state eventually decided its economy could not survive without it. That is why by 1860 nearly half the people in Alabama were slaves. It is also why Alabama refused to free the slaves when the northern states demanded it. That refusal led to the Civil War.

From 1861 until 1865, Alabama was part of the Confederate States of America. It fought many bloody battles against the armies of the North. But in the end, Alabama and the South lost. The state was then forced to free all its slaves.

For many decades after the Civil War, former slaves and their descendants were badly mistreated by the former slave owners and their descendants. It was not until the second half of the 20th century that the federal government and the courts began taking steps to stop the mistreatment.

In modern times, many whites and blacks have joined together to put this bitter past behind them. They have helped make Alabama a great state where people from all backgrounds can grow up happy.

Two friends walk together in Elsanor, Alabama. Today, people from all backgrounds help make Alabama a great state.

Did You Know?

- Most states have a tornado season. Alabama has two. Its tornadoes are among the deadliest and most destructive in the United States.

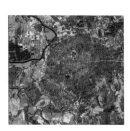

- A meteorite 1,000 feet (300 m) wide hit the earth in Alabama and left a crater 5 miles (8 km) wide. This occurred long before there were any humans. But the crater still exists. It is near the town of Wetumpka.

- The sailing ship rightfully belonging to Captain Jack Sparrow in the movie

Pirates of the Caribbean was built for Disney filmmakers at the Steiner Shipyard in Bayou La Batre, Alabama.

- Alabama is the home of Space Camp. This is a place where kids go to learn how to be astronauts and fighter jet pilots. Space Camp is run by the United States Space and Rocket Center in Huntsville, Alabama. More than 500,000 children have been to Space Camp since it started in 1982. Campers do many things there. One of the most exciting activities is to practice space missions aboard an exact copy of a space shuttle.

People

Helen Keller (1880-1968) was the first deaf and blind person to graduate from an American college. She was a baby when illness took away her hearing and sight.

Helen Keller (left) with her teacher, Anne Sullivan (right).

Keller grew to become an angry child who broke things because she could not talk to people. Her parents hired a teacher by the name of Anne Sullivan. She taught Keller to understand words through a special sign language for people who cannot see. But it was not easy for Keller to learn this language. Her story has been told in a famous stage play and movie called *The Miracle Worker*. Keller was born in Tuscumbia, Alabama.

Nat King Cole (1919-1965) was one of America's most popular entertainers. He started out playing jazz piano. Later, he became better known as a singer of pop tunes. He was also a famous songwriter. In 1956, he became the first African American to host a network TV variety show. *The Nat King Cole Show* was on NBC (National Broadcasting Company). Cole was born in Montgomery, Alabama.

Jesse Owens (1913-1980) won four gold medals in track and field at the 1936 Summer Olympic Games in Berlin, Germany. His victories were important for two reasons. First, he was very sick when he was  a child. No one expected him to grow up to be a star athlete. Second, he made Nazi German dictator Adolf Hitler look foolish. Hitler had boasted that German athletes were unbeatable because they belonged to the "master race." Hitler believed that black men like Owens were inferior and less than human. The world laughed at Hitler when Owens showed he was stronger and faster than Hitler's so-called "supermen." Owens was born near the town of Oakville, Alabama.

Harper Lee (1926-) wrote a great American novel called *To Kill a Mockingbird*. The story paints a picture of life in small-town Alabama that is both happy and sad. It is told through the eyes of a six-year-old girl whose father is a lawyer. He defends a black man falsely accused of a terrible crime. The book was published in 1960. It was later turned into an Oscar-winning movie. Lee was born in Monroeville, Alabama.

Cities

Birmingham is Alabama's largest city. Its population is 229,800. Birmingham is located in the north-central part of the state. Its nickname is the Pittsburgh of the South because for a long time it was a center of iron and steel production.

Birmingham was started in 1871 to help change Alabama from a backward farm state to an industrial powerhouse. Today, it is one of America's most important centers of commerce.

Montgomery is the capital of Alabama. With a population of 204,086, it is the state's second-largest city. Montgomery is located near the center of Alabama's southern half. It is a city with a rich history. During the Civil War, it was the first capital of the rebel Confederate states. During the middle of the 20th century, Montgomery was a birthplace of America's civil rights movement.

Civil rights marchers in March 1965.

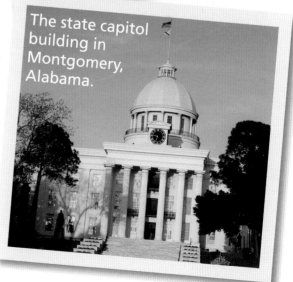
The state capitol building in Montgomery, Alabama.

Mobile is called the Port City because of its huge number of cargo ship docks. Its location on the coast of the Gulf of Mexico also makes it an important city for shipbuilding. Also, Mobile is a center for medicine, manufacturing, retail, services, aerospace, and construction. The population of Mobile is 191,411. It is Alabama's third-largest city.

Mobile is located on the Gulf of Mexico. It is called the Port City.

Huntsville is located in the northernmost part of Alabama. It has a population of 171,327. America's voyages to the moon, the planets, and the outer reaches of the solar system were all planned in Huntsville at NASA's Marshall Space Flight Center. Naturally, aerospace is Huntsville's most famous industry.

Many people in Huntsville work at NASA's Marshall Space Flight Center.

Transportation

A tugboat pushes a barge full of goods up an Alabama river.

Alabama has many inland waterways that are used for shipping. Its system of waterways is the second largest in the nation. These waterways connect Alabama to important inland ports throughout America's Midwest. Barges and small ships traveling through Alabama can come and go from three ports on the Tennessee River, two ports on the Tenn-Tom Waterway, and one port on the Alabama River. The most important port in Alabama is in Mobile. It is the state's only saltwater and deepwater port.

There are about 100 public airports in Alabama. The largest is Birmingham-Shuttlesworth International Airport. It handles about three million passengers each year. Commercial airlines fly in and out of five other Alabama airports.

Birmingham-Shuttlesworth International Airport.

A train trestle (bridge) over the Black Warrior River.

More than 3,500 miles (5,633 km) of railroad tracks crisscross Alabama. Most of those tracks are used by freight trains carrying coal.

Five major interstate highways pass through Alabama. Most of these intersect at Birmingham. Vehicles travel on more than 94,000 miles (151,278 km) of highways, streets, and roads in Alabama.

Natural Resources

About one-fourth of the land in Alabama is used for farming. Chickens are the state's most important farm product. Next in importance are cattle, flowers, and eggs. Long ago, cotton was king in Alabama. Now it is fifth in importance.

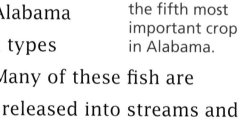

Today cotton is the fifth most important crop in Alabama.

Something else grown on Alabama farms are fish. The two main types raised are bass and catfish. Many of these fish are

Catfish in a tank at a market.

released into streams and lakes for the enjoyment of sports fishermen. Others are sent to supermarkets and restaurants.

More important is the commercial fishing industry that catches fish in the Gulf of Mexico. That industry's fleet of boats is based mainly at the port of Bayou La Batre, which is near Mobile.

Forests cover almost 23 million acres (9 million ha) of Alabama. Nearly all are privately owned. Enough trees are harvested each year to produce more than 2 billion board feet (4.7 million cbm) of softwood and hardwood lumber.

Alabama is a coal-mining state. It is also a producer of minerals such as kaolin, lime, bentonite, and iron oxide pigments.

A coal mine in Tuscaloosa, Alabama.

Industry

Alabama makes many things for the rest of the country and the world. One of the most important is automobiles. Alabama also produces steel, electronics, computer hardware, textiles, and parts for jets and rockets.

Restaurants and supermarkets are plentiful in Alabama. So are most other kinds of retail stores and shops.

A worker moves a vat of melted steel at Alabama's Birmingham Steel Corporation.

Contributing to the Alabama economy are service industries such as accounting, consulting, repair, and legal. Other important industries include construction and healthcare. All of these were kept very busy following the devastation of Hurricane Katrina in 2005. The hurricane caused millions of dollars in damage that had to be cleaned up. The storm's monster winds and lashing rain also disrupted many manufacturing activities in the western half of the state.

A bulldozer is used to clear away debris from a home in Gulf Shores, Alabama. After Hurricane Katrina in 2005, many jobs were created in the cleanup, repair, and construction industries.

Sports

There are no major league professional sports teams in Alabama. However, there are a number of minor league clubs. In baseball, there are the Birmingham Barons, Huntsville Stars, Mobile BayBears, and the Montgomery Biscuits. Low-level minor league hockey is played in Huntsville by a team called the Havoc.

Another minor league attraction in Huntsville is an arena football team known as the Tennessee Valley Vipers. Huntsville also is home to the Alabama Renegades, of the National Women's Football Association.

Sports fans can also get their fill of football action and other athletic competitions by following the college teams at Auburn University, the University of Alabama, University of Alabama at Birmingham,

Troy University, Alabama A&M University, Alabama State University, Jacksonville State University, Samford University, University of Alabama at Huntsville, or University of South Alabama.

Also popular in Alabama are the sports of roller derby and stock car racing. Roller derby teams are based in Birmingham, Huntsville, and Mobile. The most famous stock car racetrack in the state is the Talladega Superspeedway.

Several NASCAR races take place at the Talladega Superspeedway.

Entertainment

Arts and entertainment in Alabama come in all forms, shapes, and sizes. More than eight million titles of books are on the shelves of public libraries across Alabama. The Alabama Shakespeare Festival in Montgomery is one of the largest such celebrations in the world. More than 300,000 people attend. For those who enjoy fine music, there are symphony orchestras in Birmingham, Huntsville, Mobile, and Tuscaloosa, Alabama.

The state also has many museums. Its most important art museum is in Birmingham. In Mobile, a World War II battleship has been turned into a floating museum.

The battleship USS *Alabama* is a museum in Mobile, Alabama.

Outdoor events are popular in Alabama. More than 50,000 people turn out each Memorial Day weekend to see the Alabama Jubilee Hot Air Balloon Classic in the city of Decatur. The main attraction is the flight of as many as 60 balloons.

Decatur is the site of the Spirit of America Festival. This is one of the South's biggest

The Hound and Hare Balloon Race during the Alabama Jubilee.

Fourth of July celebrations. The free event features a gigantic fireworks show along with sports tournaments, parachute jumping demonstrations, pony rides, contests and games for kids, and big-name entertainment for grown-ups.

Timeline

700—The earliest people in Alabama begin building ceremonial mounds.

1400—Creek, Cherokee, and other Native American tribes begin settling in Alabama.

Hernando de Soto

1519—Spain begins exploration of Alabama. Five attempts at colonization fail.

1682—France begins exploring Alabama.

1702—France builds Europe's first successful settlement in Alabama.

1819—Alabama admitted as the 22nd state in the Union.

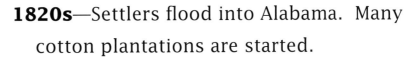

1820s—Settlers flood into Alabama. Many cotton plantations are started.

1861—Alabama joins the Confederacy to keep slavery legal. The Civil War begins.

1865—The Confederacy is defeated in the Civil War. All slaves are set free. Alabama is brought back into the Union.

1871—The city of Birmingham is founded to help Alabama build many businesses.

1950s—Movement to give blacks full equality begins and gathers strength.

1960s—Blacks win full equality with whites. Alabama becomes a center for United States missions into space.

Glossary

Civil Rights Movement—A nationwide effort beginning in the 1950s to reform federal and state laws so that blacks could enjoy full equality with whites.

Civil War—The war fought between America's Northern and Southern states from 1861-1865. The Southern states were for slavery. They wanted to start their own country. Northern states fought against slavery and a division of the country.

Dixie—A nickname for the southern region of the United States. It may have started with the drawing of boundaries between Pennsylvania and Maryland in the 1760s. The line between those colonies was created by surveyors Charles Mason and Jeremiah Dixon. It became known as the Mason-Dixon Line. People soon after began joking that everything north of that line was Mason country and everything south of it was Dixon. Dixon eventually became Dixie.

Hurricane—A violent wind storm that begins in tropical ocean waters. Hurricanes cause dangerously high tides and bring deadly waves, driving rain, and even tornadoes. Hurricanes break up and die down after reaching land.

Middle Ages—In European history, the Middle Ages were a period defined by historians as roughly between 476 AD and 1450 AD.

National Aeronautics and Space Administration (NASA)—A U.S. government agency started in 1958. NASA's goals include space exploration, as well as increasing people's understanding of Earth, our solar system, and the universe.

Plain—A large, flat area of land. There are few trees on plains. Many are filled with grasses.

Plateau—A large, flat section of land that is raised up from the surrounding countryside.

Waterway—A stream or river wide and deep enough for boats to travel along.

Index